Nature Walk

Flowers

by Rebecca Stromstad Glaser

Bullfrog Books

Ideas for Parents and Teachers

Bullfrog Books let children practice reading informational texts at the earliest reading levels. Repetition, familiar words, and photo labels support early readers.

Before Reading

- Discuss the cover photo. What does it tell them?

- Look at the picture glossary together. Read and discuss the words.

Read the Book

- "Walk" through the book and look at the photos. Let the child ask questions. Point out the photo labels.
- Read the book to the child, or have him or her read independently.

After Reading

- Prompt the child to think more. Ask: What flowers have you seen? What colors were they? How many petals did they have?

Bullfrog Books are published by Jump!
5357 Penn Avenue South
Minneapolis, MN 55419
www.jumplibrary.com

Library of Congress Cataloging-in-Publication Data
Glaser, Rebecca Stromstad.
Flowers / by Rebecca Stromstad Glaser.
p. cm. -- (Bullfrog books: nature walk)
Summary: "Describing parts of flowers and different types of flowers, this photo-illustrated nature walk guide shows very young readers how to tell the difference between flowers and other plants. Includes picture glossary"--Provided by publisher.
Includes bibliographical references and index.
ISBN 978-1-62031-024-3 (hardcover: alk. paper)
1. Flowers--Juvenile literature. I. Title.
QK49.G56 2012
580--dc23   2012009099

Series Designer   Ellen Huber
Book Designer   Ellen Huber
Photo Researcher   Heather Dreisbach

Photo Credits: Alamy, 12, 13, 23bl, 23tl; Dreamstime, 14, 15, 18, 19, 23tr; Getty Images, 18; Shutterstock, 1, 3, 4, 5, 6, 7, 8–9, 10, 11, 16, 17, 20b, 20t, 21, 22, 23br, 24

Printed in the United States of America at Corporate Graphics in North Mankato, Minnesota
7-2012/PO 1123

10 9 8 7 6 5 4 3 2 1

Table of Contents

Looking for Flowers

Let's go on a nature walk.
Do you see any flowers?

Look for colorful petals.

petal

**Petals are many colors.
A tiger lily is orange.**

Look for stems.

8

stem

A stem takes water to the flower.
Water helps flowers grow.

Look for leaves.

A leaf takes
in sunlight.

Sunlight helps
flowers grow too.

Look on trees.

Orange blossoms are white.

Blossoms grow first.
Then the fruit grows.

Look on a bush.
A wild rose is pink.

It has thorns.

Look for a butterfly.
It drinks nectar from flowers.

pollen

Look for a bee.

It gathers pollen
from flowers.

Where do you see flowers?

Parts of a Flower

petal
One of the colored outer parts of a flower.

stem
The long main part of a plant from which the leaves and flowers grow.

leaf
A flat, green part of a plant that grows from a stem.

Picture Glossary

blossom
A flower on
a fruit tree.

pollen
Tiny yellow
grains made by
flowers that help
a flower grow.

nectar
A sweet liquid
that butterflies
and bees drink
from flowers.

thorn
A sharp point
on the branch or
stem of a plant.

Index

To Learn More

Learning more is as easy as 1, 2, 3.

1) Go to www.factsurfer.com

2) Enter "flowers" into the search box.

3) Click the "Surf" button to see a list of websites.

With factsurfer.com, finding more information is just a click away.